The Doctrine of Creation

ACCORDING TO

DARWIN, AGASSIZ, AND MOSES.

BY

THE REV. JOHN KIRK,

LONDON

1869

ON THE DOCTRINE OF CREATION ACCORDING TO DARWIN, AGASSIZ, AND MOSES. *By the Rev. John Kirk, Professor of Practical Theology in the Evangelical Union Academy, Glasgow; Author of " The Age of Man Geologically considered in its bearing on the Truths of the Bible," &c., &c.; Mem. Vict. Inst.*

IT is not wonderful that men should search after the origin of earthly things, though it does seem wonderful that any should fancy that they find that origin in a *nebula*. We are accustomed to say of certain matters that they "end in smoke"; and perhaps that which has such an ending may have had an equally intangible beginning; but that a self-condensing gas should prove to have been the prime source of all which goes to make up this wondrous world, draws, we confess, too heavily on our believing powers. Such, however, is the *logical terminus* of all the evolutionary schemes of creation. We are led by them, if we are disposed to go "all the way," to imagine that all things and all beings, in the terrestrial universe at least, are but the results of self-moving "gemmules" from a luminous mist, rather than the works of an Almighty Maker.

And yet, absurd though they seem, it is, no doubt, important that we should frankly face all such notions, and put the reasonings by which men seek to sustain them to the test of sound and serious argument. To do so, we cannot rest satisfied with the teachings of what is frequently called Science, to the exclusion of that which is regarded as Philosophy. It is one of the grand delusions of a somewhat popular style of thought at the present day, that a man needs only to know " phenomena " in order to be truly intelligent in relation to nature. But the philosophy which so confines itself can have nothing to do with the origin and causes of things; neither can it throw the very least light on the nature of the changes which they undergo. The lad who marvelled that the large wheel of a coach did not run over the little one, was occupied with "phenomena," but showed true humanity in wondering after their *relations*. We must understand these relations if we would satisfy the intellect, and to do so really, we must reason about that which has all its existence in thought, as well as observe that which has its being in the material only.

It is well, therefore, in approaching a controverted scientific subject like that now before us, to note, at the outset, the fundamental principles which it involves. If our beliefs are at antipodes as to these, it is not probable that we shall reach anything like harmony, however long we may protract our discussions.

By that which is properly metaphysical reasoning, we learn that a *form* in itself is nothing. It is only a mode of existence in that substance whose form it is for the moment. When men speak of "forms" apart from individual things or beings, it should be borne in mind that they speak of that which has no existence in nature. There are material substances, each of which has its ever-changing form ; but these substances are things or beings, not forms.

A *type* in itself is nothing. It is not even a mode of existence in anything other than the mind in which it may perhaps be an idea for the time. There is nothing in nature corresponding to the word "type" as used by the naturalist. When, therefore, men speak of "types" or of "typical forms," they speak of that which really *is not*, except as a state of their own imaginations.

Life, in itself, has no separate existence, any more than form or type. It is only a state of existence in a substance which, for the time being, is alive. It is, I believe, only a state of movement. That which we call "life" in a material substance is *motion, and nothing more.* Should we use a microscope powerful enough to enable us to see those movements in certain particles of the living blood which are now called "protoplasm," and set down as "the physical basis of life"— when we perceive the wavelets within these living particles, what do we observe but *movement?* By a great magnifying power we can trace the motion into portions of the material which is alive, far beyond the point of smallness reached by the naked eye; but we see nothing then different from the larger wavelets of the great stream which passes through the heart itself. We are not one whit nearer the discovery of anything else than motion when we have got to the so-called "protoplasm" and its movements, than when we look at the entire man as he walks before us.

Force, unless the word is understood as identical with *motion*, has, to my mind, no proper place in material changes strictly so called. To say that any portion of material substance has great force is only to say in truth that it moves in a certain way, unless we mean to include more than matter in the statement. By means of those senses through which we perceive changes in material objects, we can perceive movement; but we can neither see, nor hear, nor touch, nor taste, nor smell force in the sense of that which produces movement. When Professor Huxley turns his microscope on the point of a nettle spine, he sees no *force*—he sees movement *only*. He calls the pulsating matter the protoplasm of the nettle; but it is only matter in motion and nothing more. The moment any one speaks of true force he leaves the strictly material which may be *seen*, and turns, not his eyes, but his reason to another province of being.

A *law* has no existence other than as an idea or state of the mind. There is no such substance as a law; nor is there any such quality of any substance. The word expresses no reality in nature except a state of thought, whether we look to laws written or unwritten. Written laws are ideas expressed or signified; unwritten laws are ideas unexpressed or unsignified. When any one speaks of changes effected in nature by "laws impressed on matter,"* his words have no thinkable meaning. Matter has no ideas, and therefore can have no laws so impressed on it as to affect it in any way. What are called "the immutable laws of the material universe" are nothing in reality but ideas in the minds of those who speak of them; and of all mutable things these ideas are among the most mutable. Of all confused and contradictory things, they are the most confused and self-destructive. What, for example, are Darwin's "laws of variation" but just Darwin's ideas? And, as we shall see, there is nothing among all the changing thoughts of humanity more self-contradictory than these same ideas. What are Sir Charles Lyell's laws impressed on the materials out of which the earth itself is constructed, but just the ideas of that very amiable geologist? And when we compare the first and the last of the ten editions of his "Principles," how perfectly does one set of these ideas destroy the other! But it is the same all through the wide world of what are called "laws of nature." How marvellous that men should mistake their own ever-changing notions for Divine Rule!

Uniformity represents an idea only: and when the term is used as expressive of the relation of one change to another in nature, its meaning is loose in the extreme. To a child at a certain stage of his knowledge any man is his father—a little

* Darwin's *Origin of Species*, p. 576. 1866.

further on, and only some men call forth his exclamation of
" papa !"—by-and-by only one man does so. To an untutored
observer all green things growing on the surface of a grassy
field are simply " grass "—when that same mind has learned
a little more, there are some green things that are " weeds,"
and not grass—to that mind, when highly educated botanically,
there appears a vast variety of " plants " in that field. But
to the most cultivated botanist on earth there is a variety of
constantly changing forms among these plants almost infinitely
beyond his utmost powers of discrimination. No two blades are
exactly alike, nor is one bud or seed produced with precisely
the same germinal character as another. What then does
" uniformity" mean when applied to such changes as issue in
that variety ? Only something very like that which makes a
young child call every man his father. We have the faculty
of observing certain points in nature which have a certain
degree of sameness in their relation to each other; and the
faculty is of great practical value; but it falls immeasurably
short of what those imagine who speak of *exactness* in human
thought. We shall see the bearing of such remarks as these
when we direct our attention to the much-agitated questions
that relate to the likenesses and diversities which give rise to
such abstractions as those expressed by " species " and such-
like terms.

In dealing, then, abstractly with forms, and types, and
laws of life, it is necessary to remember that we are dealing
with states of mind only. Our field is one of thoughts rather
than of things. In this field all about which we reason is
constantly and strangely changing, for all consists of the ever-
fluctuating notions of men. Certain of these notions are no
doubt called " exact science "; but there is nothing less exact
in the universe. Some of these notions are held to be "settled
points " in science ; but there is nothing less settled on earth
or anywhere else. The " form " called a " variety " to-day is a
" species " to-morrow, perhaps a " genus " next day, not
unlikely something higher next, and maybe it is back to a
" variety " again in a month ! So a fundamental law of creation
last year is a myth in the present ! This would be wonderful
if it occurred among the realities of nature, but need not
surprise us in the states of a strongly speculative mind.

This ever-fluctuating thought, too, has relation to a material
world of perpetual change. That natural history, indeed, into the
essential principles of which the scientific and philosophic inquirer is ever searching, is proceeding in a manner calculated
profoundly to increase the fluctuations of his thinkings. There
is truly immeasurable variety—incessant change. I believe

we are right when we say that no two substances in the universe have exactly the same form. Neither has the same substance had the same form twice. Neither does any substance contain the same form during two seconds of its existence. The rocks composing "the everlasting hills" themselves are undergoing incessant metamorphosis—perpetual change. That which is dead and decaying is changing as truly as that which is living and in a state of growth. When we speak of "permanent" forms or types of either the living or the dead in nature, we should remember that we are speaking of ideas only—not of actual things or beings in the natural world.

It is because of considerations like these that we are disposed to discuss certain notions as to the origin of life in a somewhat metaphysical rather than in a purely physical manner in this paper. Our aim really is to test the consistency of *thought*, rather than to follow the mere detail of fact on which that thought is so far founded. We are mistaken if in the end this mode of dealing with fanciful theories will not be found to be the most ready and efficient for the common mind. Ordinary inquirers get bewildered amid millions of facts thrown upon them as it were in cartloads, while they can trace the truth, or detect the fallacy of principles if these are fairly placed in comparison.

And yet we must remember that there is a field of fact on which the ever-fluctuating spirit broods, and in which it searches for those thoughts which constitute truth, from their being in due correspondence with the actual state of things. Among the myriads of fancies there are myriads of true ideas. The grand object of science is to gather and treasure up these. In doing so it must sift out from among heaps of chaff the true grains of reality. In order to do this it must keep close to the concrete in arguing out the abstract.

But let us take an illustration of this from that which will, at the same time, be an important step in our present inquiry. We lay hold of an individual living substance. There it is, and ideas associated with it are soon occupying our minds. That individual had a parent substance, and in thought we see that. It will itself produce, we may safely believe, as it has been produced. Let us say that it is a sapling, and grew from a seed which was the produce of a former tree. We need not go further back, at present, but rather go forward, keeping strictly in view the plant we have in hand. This, we shall say, will become a stately oak and produce acorns, which will in their turn grow into oaks and produce acorns too. Or let our example be an animal growing from an embryo produced by a former animal, and ere long to be the parent of another

embryo, or of many embryos, that will become animals and
produce other embryos in the chain of living substances, on
one link of which we have fastened for our present purpose.
Here then, we have a substance, and not an abstraction; but
we are in search of abstractions such as will stand in some true
relation to this and all kindred beings in their life-changes.
We are in search of an idea, or ideas, that will accord with that
change from which these changes started as from their true
original, and from which the constantly-changing forms of
those living substances took their character. *What shall be
the order of our inquiry?*

A *germ* is as truly a *terminus* as it is an origin. An acorn
is a *fruit* as truly as it is a seed. If we look strictly at the
chain of changes in the order of nature, the aspect in which
we see the germ as a fruit is before the seed aspect, not after
it. There is no seed which is not the result of maturity in
that whose seed it is. If we begin at our present stand-point
and go back along the chain of changes that have taken place
in the succession of any living substance we can reach no
germ which is not the result of matured growth, any more than
we can reach a matured organism which has not followed in
the wake of a germ. What good reason can any one give why
we should fancy that the origin of such a succession must be
in the seed and not in the matured individual which produced,
or so to speak, terminated in that seed? Why should men's
minds gather round *embryos* when they are in search of the
origin of beings? I can think of no satisfactory reply to such
questions.

But these give rise to other questions of similar import. It
is true that the seed is smaller than the tree—the embryo is
smaller than the matured animal; but on what ground do we
reason that small things are the originals of larger things?
Are not these small things brought forth of larger? Beyond
doubt they are. If to give being to individual living objects
be to give origin, then it is the large that give origin to the
small, not the small that originate the greater. Is there not
a radical mistake in the notion of origin that seeks for it
among infinitesimals? When men insist on finding the true
idea of the origin of things by means of the microscope, do
they not invert the order of a sound philosophy? I see no
way of escaping the conclusion that they do so. If by the
most powerful combination of light and lenses that could be
invented we should discover the minutest germ that human
eyesight can rationally hope to see, that germ would still be
the product of a larger parent; and hence the discovery would
still leave the order of nature, so far as known, to be that of

the larger giving origin to the smaller—not the smaller giving origin to the larger.

Moreover, it is not the germ that gives *character* to the matured organism—it is confessedly the matured organism that gives character to the germ. That character is *developed merely*, as the growth of the individual goes on. The "varieties," of which so much is made in this controversy, are accounted for, by Darwin himself, chiefly not by their being traced to their embryos, but beyond these to affections of the matured organs of reproduction. It is by these affections of the matured organs that he regards these varieties as originating in the germ or embryo.* This is, beyond question, finding the origin of character in the parent, and not in the embryo. Why then should originals be sought for in embryonic littleness and not in matured greatness?

It is quite true that the individual, *when once originated,* is developed from small to great; but philosophy is not, in this matter, in search of growth or development, but of *origin.* Whether we are bent on finding the true idea as to the beginning of individuals, or of kinds, we seem to be carried beyond germs and into parents. Once having got the germs, we have no difficulty as to their growth. The character of the germ determining all the great features of the individual to be developed from it, but not determining the character of the next germ in succession, we are driven away from germs in looking for origin. The reproductive organs being affected, not by germinal character, but by external conditions acting upon them, and only through them on the germ, compels us to seek the first link in the chain of being in the mature producer, and not in the germinal or embryonic product. What will a philosopher of the popular school say to this?

Here, however, we come somewhat more directly on the ideas of Darwin. His theory of origin, which he calls "Pangenesis," is founded (perhaps to him unconsciously, but really founded) on that of the matured organism originating the germ and giving it all its character. His ideas are inconsistent with the germ's originating or giving character to the matured being. He puts his theory himself in these words:—"The whole organization," he says, "in the sense of every separate atom or unit, reproduces itself." The ovule or seed, under this notion, consists of multitudinous gemmules "thrown off from each separate atom of the organism."† We shall see the inherent absurdity of this theory afterwards;

* See *Origin of Species*, p. 8. 1866.
† *The Variation of Animals and Plants under Domestication*, p. 358. 1868.

meanwhile, it is clear that it proceeds upon the principle that the germ receives its being and character entirely from the matured organism, and is inconsistent with any thought of the germ giving origin or character to the matured being. It is not possible on such a theory to follow the chain of things logically backward to a real origin which shall not be a parent rather than a germ. This, moreover, is in perfect accordance with Nature's own order. However inconsistent, Darwin is right so far here.

But we come now to another of this great naturalist's ideas of origin. We may quote the whole passage, in which it is most clearly expressed. He says :—

It is interesting to contemplate an entangled bank, clothed with many plants of many kinds, with birds singing on the branches, with various insects flitting about, and with worms crawling through the damp earth, and to reflect that these elaborately constructed forms, so different from each other, and dependent on each other in so complex a manner, have all been produced by laws acting around us. These laws, taken in the largest sense, being growth with reproduction ; inheritance which is almost implied by reproduction ; variability from the indirect and direct actions of the external conditions of life, and from use and disuse ; a ratio of increase so high as to lead to a struggle for life, and as a consequence, to natural selection, entailing divergence of character and the extinction of less-improved forms. Thus from the war of nature, from famine and death, the most exalted object that we are capable of conceiving, namely, the production of the higher animals, directly follows. There is a grandeur in this view of life, with its several powers having been originally breathed, by the Creator, into a few forms, or into one ; and that while this planet has gone cycling according to the fixed law of gravity, from so simple a beginning, endless forms most beautiful and most wonderful have been, and are being evolved.*

It is not easy to see what Darwin here means by " a few forms," or by " one." If he mean anything real, he must speak of substances—actual living creatures. If he does mean actual plants or animals, or a plant or an animal, what kind of a plant or animal was this into which the Creator breathed originally these " several powers " ? It is very clear that it must have been a parent plant or a parent animal. From it, according to Pangenesis, innumerable " gemmules " must have gone off to form the first seed or egg, which it produced " after its kind." But what must that " kind " have been ? Darwin says it was " simple " ! Pangenesis insists that gemmules of all in a germ must have been either in the parent of that germ, or in some of the progenitors of that parent; and so atoms of all that belongs to all that have come, or will yet come, from this original "form," must have been there! If this should be admitted as among the possibilities of fancy, how then could this "form" be *simple?*

But we are no less at a loss with another element in this theory of creation. There are "several powers" that are "breathed" into this inexplicable creature that formed the parent of all else. What does this mean? We can fancy motion as the result of breathing; and if any one chooses to call this motion "force," I have no very strong objection to the word, for it is still understood as only motion. But when a substance (shall we say a minute jelly-fish?) is said to be "breathed into," and thereby rendered capable of exerting such "powers" as have produced all the variety of living Nature, I confess to a feeling of bamboozlement. If we must accept Pangenesis, with its myriad atoms, each capable of the amazing power (for an atom!) of throwing off ever so many more atoms or gemmules, but, after all, go back to the Creator's breathing powers into organized beings, rendering the first capable of creating all the rest, are we not indulging in very incoherent dreams? I can easily understand what is meant by God's giving that movement which we call life, under the expressive figure of breathing into objects otherwise stagnant; but it is quite a different thing to understand His breathing into a simple substance so as to give it the power of transforming itself into all the varieties of the living world. To give movement, and to give power to regulate and sustain movement, constitute the subjects of two most distinct ideas. To give such movement as even a cell with life possesses, and to give such powers as could regulate and increase that movement so as to issue in the immense results that form the subject-matter of the natural history of earth, are thoughts almost infinitely at opposites. I feel, indeed, as if it were hard to believe that Darwin *thought* what he wrote when he penned the words on which we are remarking.

This appears all the more difficult of belief when we turn to his ideas at another point. He says,—"Some authors believe it to be as much the function of the reproductive system to produce individual differences, or very slight deviations of structure, as to make the child like its parents." This Darwin proceeds to modify, and says "that the reproductive system is eminently susceptible to changes in the conditions of life; and to this system being functionally disturbed in the parents I chiefly attribute the varying or plastic conditions of the offspring."* Here Darwin represents "some authors" as believing that which is indeed the natural result of his own theory of creation. If a parent creature had certain powers breathed into it, such as could regulate and determine future varieties, then it must be the function of the reproductive system in that creature to produce differences of all sorts. But this is just what he proceeds to disprove! It is not by the powers breathed into the producer, but by the functional disturbance of the reproductive system, and that through means external to the creature altogether, that the varieties are caused! Elsewhere he speaks of the effect produced on the growing individual by external circumstances; but when we carefully follow out his ideas, it is by the effect of those circumstances on the reproductive system, and through that on inheritance, that these circumstances have any influence in giving rise to variations. This throws us back again on the theory of Pangenesis.

Observe Darwin's own illustration of the working of this imaginary law. He says,—" If one of the simplest Protozoa be formed, as it appears under the microscope, of a small mass of homogeneous gelatinous matter, a minute atom thrown off from any part and nourished under favourable circumstances would naturally reproduce the whole; but if the upper and lower surfaces were to differ in texture from the central portion, then all three parts would have to throw off atoms or gemmules, which when aggregated by natural affinity would form either buds or the sexual elements." † In what way could external conditions, then, account for variations in the forms of life? If the "form" which was first created was like the first example here supposed, and hence " simple," by what conceivable condition could it be made to give origin to the second " form"? That requires three sorts of " atoms," but this has only one sort. We could hold to this pangenesis only by believing that the first forms, instead of being simple, were infinitely complex!

But let us take another of his illustrations. He says,—" I presume that no physiologist doubts that, for instance, each bone-corpuscle of the finger differs from the corresponding corpuscle in the corresponding joint of the toe; and there can hardly be a doubt that even those on the corresponding sides of the body differ, though almost identical in nature. This near approach to identity is curiously shown in many diseases in which the same exact points on both sides of the body are similarly affected." ‡ It is here very evident that there is one

---

* *Origin of Species*, pp. 157, 158.
† *Variation of Plants, &c.*, vol. ii. p. 376.   ‡ Ibid. vol. ii. p. 369.

great truth which Darwin overlooks in the construction of his theory. In carrying out his idea of innumerable atoms such as would fly, each to its respective bone or part of a bone, or any other part of the material body, he speaks of the smallness of the atoms of the virus of small-pox that convey the disease, and of the small portions of diseased mucus from a plague-stricken ox, which is sufficient to corrupt the whole mass of a healthy animal when introduced into its blood; and he says,—"The organic particles with which the wind is tainted over miles of space by certain offensive animals must be infinitely minute and numerous, yet they strongly affect the olfactory nerves."* But there are no such particles, any more than there are "organic particles" in the sounds that affect the auditory nerves. He is dreaming of the old notion that led men to calculate all the "imponderables;" such as how light a bushel of smell must be when a rose could give off as much as would fill and refill a large hall with that material for weeks or months together! He forgets that all such notions are banished from tolerably informed minds, and that smells, like sounds, consist of movements only. What is necessary but a movement of a peculiar kind given to the particles of the blood or to the substance of the sympathetic nerves of the living body in order to the plague itself? The electric shock we now know does not discharge particles of some peculiar substance called "the fluid of electricity" through that body which is rendered a lifeless mass by it in less than a second of time. It communicates only such a motion as absorbs that other motion which we call Life, and leaves that stagnation which we call Death. But Mr. Darwin, apparently, does not see this; and hence his resort to infinitely numerous atoms, together with all the inconsistency into which these lead him.

When we follow this naturalist into the region of true natural history we find that his notions lack evidence, as they lack coherence when we compare them among themselves. In doing so it is necessary to keep in mind that it is not the mere meaning of the word "species" after which Darwin is really in search. Neither is it the mere development of one species from another, when he has determined that "species" and "variety" are identical in nature. In order to discover anything to the purpose of his theory, he must point out some such way back in the history of actual living creatures as can truthfully enable us to connect them (through natural generation) with similar creatures that lived in other ages; so that, comparing these two sets of beings, we shall have proof that there has been an ad-

---

* *Var. of Plants, &c.*, vol. ii. p. 403.

vance in the scale of life somewhat like that by which an ape would prove the progenitor of a man, or, if you will, that by which a lowly savage would prove to have been the ancestor of the highly endowed among men at the present time.

Mr. Darwin (we may say of necessity) appeals to geology in favour of his system; and here too he finds "the most obvious and serious objections" to his theory.* But I humbly think that he misses that point of truth recorded by the rocks which fatally affects that theory. He dwells upon the "imperfections of the geological records," as accounting for the absence of "intermediate forms." But that merely negative matter would be no objection at all if we had evidence of *that gradation in any one form* which is really essential to the truthfulness of evolutionary ideas. For example, if the most "unequivocally ancient" of human remains indicated such a type as that from which, in the course of countless ages, man might have been improved up to his present form, we should care very little for "intermediate links." But as Sir Charles Lyell so candidly tells us, the most ancient human skull discovered, belonging, according to most geologists, to long-past ages, is equal to the average of the best-developed variety of man now existing. That skull proves that man has neither grown stronger in muscle, nor better in brain, during all those ages; and indicates that, if anything, he has degenerated in physical development if not in intellectual also.† Then the same thing is true of all other forms as it is of that of man. To take the eozoön itself, the earliest of all discovered life among foraminifers, it is a giant, and of the grandest character among its kind. So is it with gigantic but extinct species in general. "Intermediate forms," if discovered in ever so great an abundance, go for nothing, so long as the most ancient found are as highly developed as those now living in the same circumstances.

Even in the recent field of domestication, of which Mr. Darwin makes so much, it is highly questionable whether "improvement," in the sense of increased usefulness to man, is not degeneration in the sense of Nature. It is beyond question that a great many of what are called "improved breeds" are only helpless monstrosities apart from excessive human care. It is unphilosophical in the extreme to regard such monstrosities as developments of the higher from the lower in Nature's sense. There is, no doubt, variation to the utmost, but it is not variation this theory requires—it is development of higher from lower forms. And this is just the idea which all Nature's records refuse to sanction.

* *Origin of Species*, p. 340.
† See *Antiquity of Man*, p. 89. 1863.

The lapse of time does not aid the theory in the very slightest degree. If you could prove that an eternity had fled since the first man whose skull has turned up was a living inhabitant of earth, it would only make the case so much the worse for evolution, if that skull is as fully developed as the average of skulls are now. So if you prove that in a few years long-horned oxen have been changed into a polled breed, the shortness of the time proves no more than its length, unless the polled, for Nature's use, are superior to the long-horned. There must be, in the great sum of change, evidence of such an advance as that by which, through slow degrees, the first "few simple forms" have improved up to that of man. But such evidence is utterly wanting.

When we estimate fairly the amount of Darwin's teaching, it is comprised within very narrow limits. He, no doubt, greatly reduces the number of imaginary "species," and correspondingly increases that of "varieties." If any one should take it into his head to count every variety of pigeons, for example, a distinct species having its representative, not in the common root of *Columba livia*, but in a special creation of its own, such a fancy would be effectually demolished by Darwin's reasoning. So, probably, it would happen with a similar fancy in relation to dogs. If any one should insist that each variety of elephants had its separate creation, then our author would probably refute him thoroughly. If we regard the multitude of so-called "species" to which this sifting process would apply, the sweep of the system of thought wrought out by Darwin is very wide; but if we regard the system itself, it lies, as it were, in a nutshell. It means only that varieties have been in many cases mistaken for true species.

And yet Darwin's system is of no small value, so far as it truthfully goes. We feel ourselves irresistibly drawn by it greatly nearer to the comprehensive statements of Sacred Scripture, in which the species, or "kinds," are placed before us as at first less numerous than, but for Darwin's reasonings, we should be tempted to regard them in reality. He narrows, beyond doubt, the original field of creation, as that is contended for by naturalists of an opposite school; and so far he does real, though, it would seem, unconscious, service to the Bible.

But when we follow this naturalist on to the point at which he not only lessens the vast number of species, but proceeds to establish the doctrine of an all but universal evolution, we need have no difficulty in perceiving his utter lack of evidence. There is no such thing as a fragment of proof such as would show improvement of form. On the contrary, there is only too strong evidence of the opposite, especially so far as the nations of men are concerned. What is wanted, as we have said, is progression in "kinds"—shell-fish, if you will, improving into higher shell-fish—not dwindling and dying out, but rising to higher forms of molluscous being. There is the chalk of what geologists have gloried in as the *Cretaceous Period*—placing it back ever so many ages—going on now at the bottom of the North Sea; and the chalk-forming creatures exactly of the same standing in nature as they ever were.* Is this evolution? Assuredly it is not. If we look to apes, how is it that there is just as little sign of evolution among them as there is in the lowest of creation? It is not the silly talk in which men describe, in fancy, all the process by which an ape becomes a man; it is some sign of such an improvement actually going on among the simian race that we must seek. We seek in vain. But enough, for the present, on the ideas of Darwin.

I am endeavouring to keep closely in view that we are at present dealing with ideas rather than with things. As we have seen, "forms," "types," "force," "life," "law," and all the other words that go to make up the vocabulary of abstract thinking, are representative of states of mind only. "Varieties," "species," "genera," are all expressive of ideas, and nothing more. The truth of this comes very strongly upon us when we pass from one great school of thought to another and opposite school. "Forms" have no longer the same significance—"types" mean totally different abstractions,—"Life," with all its "forces," "laws," "uniformities," and "designs," is utterly diverse from what it was among the ideas which we have left. This is a matter of very great moment to the inquirer after truth. It reminds him that he ought never to confound ideas with things. He may take all the help that ideas can render; but, after all, he must seek thoughts for himself, in the way of observing Nature, and also in that of sifting most carefully the observations and reasonings of others.

When we pass from the teachings of Darwin to those of the equally celebrated Agassiz, the contrast of thought is very striking. Here "species" are no longer "improved varieties" that have diverged from each other in the course of countless ages, and in their descent from a common parentage, but "*primordial forms.*" Agassiz adopts the idea of Morton, and declares his full belief that species are thus "primordial."† "Species," he says, "are, then, distinct

---

* See Dr. Carpenter's Report, given in *Scientific Opinion*, vol. 1, p. 231.
† See *Types of Mankind*, p. lxxix. 1865.

forms of organic life, the origin of which is lost in the primitive establishment of the state of things now existing; and varieties are such modifications of the species as may return to the typical form under temporary influences." When lecturing to his associates, on his way to Brazil, he said,—"I am often asked what is my chief aim in this expedition to South America? No doubt, in a general way, it is to collect materials for future study. But the conviction which draws me irresistibly is, that the combination of animals on this continent, where the faunæ are so characteristic and so distinct from all others, will give me the means of showing that the transmutation theory is wholly without foundation in fact."* It was the full belief of Agassiz, when he had completed his journey, that his observations had more than established this conviction. There is great vigour in the faith of this distinguished naturalist; and hence the conflict of thought between those who think with Darwin and those who think with Agassiz is real and hearty. When putting the question as to whether there is any *standard* in nature by which species may be infallibly marked off from mere varieties, he says,—"The true principle of classification exists in Nature herself, and we have only to decipher it." Then he says,—"The standard is to be found in the changes animals undergo, from their first formation in the egg to their adult condition."† He notices the remarkable similarity in the embryological forms of widely differing species, and the use which a Darwinian is disposed to make of it. "But," says he, "when we follow it out in the growth of the animals themselves, and find that, close as it is, no animal ever misses its true development, or grows to anything but what it was meant to be, we are forced to admit that the gradations which unquestionably unite all animals is an intellectual, not a material one. As the works of a human intellect are bound together by mental kinship, so are the thoughts of the Creator spiritually united."‡ These are very different ideas, indeed, from those of Darwin. Even as to the process of development, their ideas are wide apart. Agassiz says, that however the processes of development "may approach or even cross each other, they never end in making any living being different from the one which gave it birth, though in reaching that point it may pass through phases resembling other animals."§—"So-called varieties or breeds," he says, "far from indicating the beginning of new types, or

---

* *Travels in Brazil*, p. 33. 1868.   † Ibid. pp. 20, 21.
‡ Ibid. pp. 22, 23.   § Ibid. p. 41. •

the initiating of new species, only point out the range of flexibility in types, which in their essence are invariable."*

It will be readily seen, from the quotations thus before us, that the ideas of Agassiz are utterly irreconcileable with those of Darwin. The latter sees the evolution of all nature's variety from atoms, or gemmules thrown off by atoms, which find their own way to their respective places in organic substances through those " several powers " that were breathed into the few original forms, or into the one original, at the beginning of life. He imagines material being to be self-moving—self-organizing—though not quite self-creating. Agassiz sees all matter only plastic in the power of an omnipresent, ever-working mind. To Darwin, matter is force; to Agassiz, mind alone is force. It is not that the two naturalists believe in the same power doing the same work, only that they differ as to the way in which it is done. " Powers," in Darwin's mind are those of material substance; in the view of Agassiz, they are those of spiritual substance. " Evolution," on the theory of Darwin, must appear the grossest absurdity to Agassiz, as it may well do to any one who looks into the real principles of life as a true philosophy reveals them.

Darwin sees no definite *idea*—indeed, no *idea whatever*—in the working out of the great natural processes. Variation with him is a matter of the purest chance, giving permanent existence to certain forms only because these happen to be the most suited to the conditions amid which the merest accident throws them ! Agassiz sees a thinking mind, with a clear plan from the first, working out that plan steadily through all the history of being. He seems to have no more thought of Scripture than Darwin ; but, deep in the foundations of his thinking, the Infinite One has such a place as constrains him ever to see that Almighty Spirit as not only the first, but the constant cause of the great harmonies of life.

Agassiz sees that this Infinite One has such a place as is inconsistent utterly with the theory of evolution. On this point he is at antipodes with Darwin. He sees *species among mankind*, as clearly defined as among any other of the genera of earth. He imagines a considerable number of creations of " first parents " for the human race, as well as for other races, each pair made suitable to a particular " province," and placed there along with suitable types of life associated with them. He says,—" The diversity among animals is a fact determined by the will of the Creator, and their geographical distribution part of the general plan which unites all organized beings

* *Travels in Brazil*, p. 42.

into one great organic conception; whence it follows that what are called human races, down to their specialization as nations, are distinct primordial forms of the type of man."* Starting from a period when he holds that this globe was unsuited to the existence of life, he says (logically enough) that when this ceased and life began, origin by development was impossible, because there were no "ancestors" from which living creatures could be developed. Here Darwin admits the creation of "a few forms, or one," into which "several powers" were "originally breathed." But Agassiz insists on the continued action, not of these powers, in which he has no faith, but of that power which gave origin to all primordial beings. He says, "Until we have some facts to prove that the power, whatever it was, which originated the first animals, has ceased to act, I can see no reason for referring the origin of life to any other cause." † By the "origin of life" here he cannot mean the first animals created merely. He clearly means the origin of life in every individual creature. It is in such ideas we see the immense divergence of his thoughts from those of Darwin; and here, I must confess, I cordially agree with Agassiz. I am not sure about his "evidence" of a state of the earth when it was impossible for living beings of any sort to exist on it; but I am fully convinced with him that there was a time when life began, and *that He who gave it origin gives it continuity.*

But now comes the testing point in the doctrine of Agassiz, when he divides the human family into distinct species, and seeks to place his proof for this division before us. In the *Types of Mankind,* by Nott and Gliddon, from which we have already quoted, we are furnished with a chart drawn up according to instructions from Agassiz. The forms of life on earth are there placed under eight heads, and the chief types are arranged in eight columns. But, in the construction of these columns, the "facts" are handled in a manner fitted to destroy all confidence in the representations of scientific men.

Here we have Africa and its typical "negro." We should expect to find the figure of an African head placed at the top of the African column to be as near the average as that adopted in the case of the other typical creatures given in the column; but no. The very lowest specimen that could be found is exaggerated into a caricature of lowness, and given as the "type"! I have seen Charles Livingstone's photographs of Africans taken in their native wilds, and he has personally told me that they were fair average heads. They would be

* *Types of Mankind,* p. 76.   † *Travels in Brazil,* p. 43.

fair average heads among ourselves! They demonstrate that this bust published by Nott and Gliddon is a shameful misrepresentation.

If we pass from this "typical" African to the "typical" European, we find the bust of Cuvier himself given as that "type." One of the very greatest men of which any country can boast, and that, too, evidently after he had lost his teeth, so that he presents the greatest possible contrast to the "prognathous" negro, is placed in comparison with the lowest form that could be selected from among the blacks. Is this science? or is it likely to lead any one to respect the honour of scientific men? The united testimony of Dr. Livingstone and his brother, in reference to their observation of natives in Africa, is this. They say, "We have seen nothing to justify the notion that they are of a different 'breed' or 'species' from the most civilized. The African is a man with every attribute of human kind."* Nor is this a testimony in favour of a mere unsupported opinion. The figures from photographs taken in the interior,—figures of men, women, and children given with the greatest fidelity, as any one may see who compares the engravings with the photographs from which they are copied,—are the most unexceptionable evidence of the truthfulness of this testimony in favour of African manhood. If men form a set of ideas in which all Europeans are Cuviers, and all Africans are like this caricature of a negro given in Nott and Gliddon's chart, what may be expected as to the conclusions to which such notions will lead them?

But there is another way in which this chart of life may be dealt with. Under each human head is a column formed of typical animals, such as are associated with the "typical" men in their several "provinces." At the foot of that of which Cuvier is the head, is the old ox of Europe (*Bos Urus*). At the foot of that headed by the Negro is the giraffe. Could Agassiz show as clear a distinction between even the caricature of the black and the portrait of Cuvier as there is between the ox and the giraffe, there might be some reason for his suggesting that the two belonged to separate primordial forms; but, with all the flagrant unfairness of the figures chosen, he can do nothing of the kind.

What then does Agassiz teach us? He stands opposed to Darwin, as we have seen, in an extreme degree; and I humbly think that he strips that naturalist of no small amount of his fancies. In his views of the localization of forms of life, together with the multitude of facts by which he establishes

* *The Zambese and its Tributaries*, p. 596.

these views, he seems to me to demonstrate that, from the first, its great specific distinctions were radical and determined —that each species, properly so called, was as perfect at the outset as it is now. Geologically he has an immense advantage over Darwin; and this advantage increases as discovery goes on. The oldest creatures are no longer regarded as having had simple organizations, that is, by well-informed geologists. As the abodes of living substances become more and more explored, too, the old notions of a gradation from small to great, and from low to high, are being dissolved. Agassiz speaks strongly in this line of thought. He says: "There are other animals in Brazil, low in their class to be sure, but yet very important to study embryologically, on account of their relation to extinct types. These are the sloths and armadillos—animals of insignificant size in our days, but anciently represented in gigantic proportions. The Megatherium, the Mylodon, the Megalonyx, were some of those immense mammoths. I believe that the embryonic changes of the sloths and armadillos will explain the structural relations of these huge Edentata and their connection with the present ones. South America teems with the fossil bones of these animals, which, indeed, penetrated into the northern half of the hemisphere as high up as Georgia and Kentucky, where their remains have been found."* It would be very difficult to find evidence of the evolution of greater from smaller, or of higher from lower forms, in such a field as Agassiz thus rapidly surveys. If evolution is there at all, it is of small from large, and low from high.

It is thus that the ideas of these two great men neutralize the extravagances of each, and throw out the truth between them. The careful study of both leads to the belief of neither of their systems fully; and yet it leads to the perception of that grand doctrine which may be said to find a resting-place partly in both. In their almost incredible researches, these men have each seen something true; and they have each, too, fancied something untrue; but when the chaff is blown off, and the good grain gathered, it will mingle harmoniously and yield a satisfactory faith.

And what shall that faith be? Shall it be that taught by Moses in the Book of God? It is not unfrequently said that the Bible was not meant to teach us science. Perhaps there is a sense in which the statement is true; but such is not the sense in which it is frequently used. When, for example, it is insisted that the Book of Genesis is not to be at all

---

* *Travels in Brazil*, pp. 24, 25.

considered in a scientific discussion on creation, and this negation is upheld by the statement in question, it is untrue. What are those grand philosophic principles around which the labours of Darwin and Agassiz gather? They are those very principles laid down with divine simplicity and truthfulness in the Bible. Let us glance at them.

There is "the beginning:" And do not both the great naturalists before us found all their speculations on this very idea of a beginning? There, again, is the chaotic state, in which life was not;—and do not both recognize this? They at least fancy that they find "scientific" evidence of it; and, whether real or fanciful, they hold the idea as an essential part of their natural philosophy. There, again, are the separations of the atmosphere from the watery surface, and of the dry land from the ocean; and assuredly we have principles of natural science there. More than geology, with the aid of all the other sciences involved, has yet wrought out, is thus laid down clear and full in the Bible. It is too bad to say that this is not meant to teach us natural science, when so-called science has failed to bring us near to the point of knowledge at which this Book places the humblest reader! But here comes the order of life, and vegetation covers the land. That vegetation is divided into such as propagates itself by its rootlets, and that which does so by its seed-bearing powers. It is not the seed, nor the budding rootlets that come first in order, but those plants which so propagate themselves, each "after its kind." Darwin would take this creation in a more limited sense than Agassiz; but both hold "inheritance" as of the last importance in the science of life. Both really accept this fundamental teaching of Moses, given so long before their day.

Then come the fishes and amphibious creatures of the waters, including fowl that fly in the air as well as live on sea and land. Is not this in strictly scientific order? If Moses did not mean to teach us science, it is surely marvellous that he taught us such perfect knowledge of nature without meaning it! If unconsciously he taught that which has never been excelled by the best minds on earth, it would be miraculous indeed. Then come before us the "great whales" of our common version, but really the gigantic originals of that vast variety of large creatures which still inhabit the earth, though now reduced to narrower dimensions. In these we are presented with neither the "few forms" of Darwin, nor with the multitudinous creations of Agassiz; yet with that very golden mean in which the truth is so often found.

I confess that I feel the very gravest doubt as to whether

the fundamental elements of all popular natural science are not merely the unconsciously retailed ideas of the Bible. I am not able to find evidence of a "beginning" in *geology*. The "nebular hypothesis," as it is called, is absurdity itself when tried by actual facts. The igneous condition of the interior of our globe, and its cooling down to its present state, is utterly inconsistent with the strongest geological evidence.* It does seem as if our great scientific men were deluding themselves with the idea that they have found in the records of the rocks that which they would never have dreamed but for their Bibles. These Bibles have taught them all the true doctrine of creation they yet know !

See how this is confirmed when we come to the creation of man. Here is a breathing into one form, not of " several powers," but of a *special life*. This is in perfect accordance with all that true science teaches, though not the result of unaided human inquiry such as claims the monopoly of being that science. In the lowest specimen of human kind there is a life, or movement, of spirit that is specific in the highest sense of the term—a movement which rises to the Creator Himself, and marks Him out as the object of either love or fear—a movement which has nothing analogous to it in all the rest of creation. Surely the teaching of such a truth in the creation of man is teaching the very loftiest and most trustworthy of all science. Compare it with the Pangenesis of Darwin, and how vastly superior is the teaching ! Compare it with the absurd representation of heads by Agassiz, and how infinitely more powerful is its self-evidence than all his fancies on the many human creations ! I must say that it seems to need only that one fairly compare this Sacred Truth with that which sets up as its rival, in order to his feeling the innermost depths of his intellectual being reached with the conviction that Moses wrote as the taught of God.

The Rev. WALTER MITCHELL, M.A., Vice-President, in closing the discussion, delivered the following Address :—

It now only remains for me to express my general concurrence with the whole argument of this admirable paper, with the exception, perhaps, of the argument on life. So far as the general scope of the paper is concerned,

---

* "The doctrine, therefore, of the pristine fluidity of the interior of the earth, and the gradual solidification of its crust consequent on the loss of internal heat by radiation into space, is one of many scientific hypotheses which has been adhered to after the proofs by which it was at first supported have given way one after the other."—*Principles of Sir Charles Lyell*, p. 211, edition 1868.

nothing could have been more admirable or convincing. A more logical paper could not have been written to expose the absurdity of Darwin's two theories, and to show how utterly impossible it is, by any logical process whatever, to reconcile them. That, then, must be a sufficient excuse for our now reconsidering the subject of Darwinism, for since our first two papers on the subject were read and discussed here, Mr. Darwin has set forth his new theory of pangenesis. It is only right that that new theory should be met and argued upon, and that it should be shown how utterly irreconcilable it is with his first theory. Illogical and untenable as his first theory was, he has now utterly destroyed it by the succeeding theory which he put forward to bolster it up. We are often told that no scientific man believes anything but this, or that no scientific man believes anything but that, and that scientific men do not believe in the history of creation as set forth in the beginning of Genesis. But here we have a convincing proof that scientific men as eminent, and naturalists as eminent, in every degree as Mr. Darwin himself are altogether at issue with his theories of creation, and that entirely upon scientific grounds. I think Professor Kirk has done well in coming in as a moderator between Agassiz, who is an eminent naturalist, as eminent as Darwin, and Mr. Darwin. He shows you that, with all their philosophy and all their science, they have not been able to make a single step in advance of the science which is to be found in the very early chapters of the book of Genesis, which we have lately been told were nothing more than the imaginings of a Hebrew Descartes. I think Professor Kirk's passages with regard to life are important, because they have a bearing on what has been put forward by Professor Huxley on the same subject. The peculiar notion which Professor Kirk seems to have of life is that it is essentially motion, and nothing but motion. He says :—

" The electric shock we now know does not discharge particles of some peculiar substance, called 'the fluid of electricity,' through that body which is rendered a lifeless mass by it in less than a second of time. It communicates only such a motion as absorbs that other motion which we call Life, and leaves that stagnation which we call Death."

Then he has another passage very much in the same way :—

" This is in perfect accordance with all that true science teaches, though not the result of unaided human inquiry, such as claims the monopoly of being that science. In the lowest specimen of human kind there is a life, or movement of spirit that is specific in the highest sense of the term—a movement which rises to the Creator Himself, and marks Him out as the object of either love or fear."

From these passages I believe Professor Kirk has some peculiar notions of that motion which he calls life, and no doubt he does hold that motion to be something essentially and totally distinct from inanimate motion, or the motion of inanimate matter. That, I think, is fully borne out by another passage, which better explains his meaning :—

"I am not sure about his 'evidence' of a state of the earth when it was impossible for living beings of any sort to exist on it ; but I am fully convinced with him that there was a time when life began, and that He who gave it origin gives it continuity."

I am afraid that perhaps Mr. Kirk has narrowed his subject somewhat too much by the endeavour to make it purely metaphysical. He has unconsciously followed in the same track, traversed in another way by Professor Huxley, who, in the current number of the *Fortnightly Review*, has given a paper on "The Physical Basis of Life," or "protoplasm," which paper contains the substance of one of the Sunday evening lectures, delivered in Edinburgh to teach men science, "in order to take away some portion of the ignorance and misery existing in the world." When we see such an announcement we are curious to ascertain what is the sort of Sunday teaching which these men are taught in order to take away that ignorance and remedy that misery. But what do I find the whole of that teaching, so far as this particular lecture is concerned, to be ? Simply this, that if you go into the lowest forms of life, whether you find it in the sting of the nettle or in the humblest forms of vegetable life, which indeed you can hardly call life except for its motion and powers of propagation, and when you ultimately get down to the very lowest form of life—to the living being, which is the very nearest approach to that which is not living—you come to what Professor Huxley calls "protoplasm," which, a little while ago, was only known as the homogeneous fluid lining the inside of the cell of a plant. We are now taught that that is "the physical basis of life ; " that there is not one single particle of our whole body, or of any part of our body, which was not, at one time or other, a protoplasm, and that that is the essential unity of life found pervading all creation. Then he goes on to tell us that there are two kinds of this protoplasm : there is the protoplasm which the plant elaborates out of the mineral kingdom, and the protoplasm which the animal elaborates out of the protoplasm of the plant. The animal cannot elaborate protoplasm out of the mineral elements of the earth at all. That may be all very true so far as the analysis of the dissecting-knife and the microscope may go, but Professor Huxley makes a great jump from that, and tells his auditors that that protoplasm—and, by the way, it is very hard to find the meaning of Greek words of that kind, especially when a literal translation gives no idea of the thing which is meant—he tells his auditors that that protoplasm is nothing more than a combination of carbon, hydrogen, oxygen, and nitrogen in some complicated form—

Mr. REDDIE.—As to the meaning of the word, it may be a misprint for protoplasti.

The CHAIRMAN.—He tells us that the chemists have not yet got the proper proportions of these elements, but that if you want to find a good equivalent for protoplasm you will find it in the white of egg, and you may be satisfied that all the elements of your body are to be found in a little smelling-salts dissolved in water ! (Laughter.) "Here you are, all masses of changed protoplasm !" (Laughter.) But we want to know what that mysterious thing called life is, because even Professor Huxley cannot get out of the habit of talking of "living beings," and "organic and inorganic matter." What I complain of Professor Huxley is, that while he tells his auditors that living protoplasm differs in no degree from the dead carbon, oxygen, hydrogen, &c., of which it is formed, except in the nature of the chemical combinations of those elements and in their proportions, he also assures them that there is no such thing as vitality existing in nature ; and that which we call vitality— all the movements we see under the microscope—are nothing more than the action of those ordinary molecular forces which reside in the elements carbon, hydrogen, nitrogen, &c. The passage is a very strong one. Professor Huxley says :—

"When hydrogen and oxygen are mixed in a certain proportion and an electric spark is passed through them they disappear, and a quantity of water, equal in weight to the sum of their weights, appears in their place. There is not the slightest parity between the passive and active powers of the water and those of the oxygen and hydrogen which have given rise to it. At 32° Fahrenheit, and far below that temperature, oxygen and hydrogen are elastic gaseous bodies, whose particles tend to rush away from one another with great force. Water, at the same temperature, is a strong though brittle solid, whose particles tend to cohere into different geometrical shapes, and sometimes build up frosty imitations of the most complex forms of vegetable foliage. Nevertheless, we call these and many other strange phenomena the properties of the water, and we do not hesitate to believe that in some way or another they result from the properties of the component elements of the water. We do not assume that a something called 'aquosity' entered into and took possession of the oxide of hydrogen as soon as it was formed and then guided the aqueous particles to their places in the facets of the crystal, or amongst the leaflets of the hoar-frost. On the contrary, we live in the hope and in the faith that, by the advance of molecular physics, we shall by-and-by be able to see our way as clearly from the constituents of water to the properties of water, as we are now able to deduce the operations of a watch from the form of its parts, and the manner in which they are put together. Is the case in any way changed when carbonic acid, water, and ammonia disappear, and in their place, under the influence of pre-existing living protoplasm, an equivalent weight of the matter of life makes its appearance ? It is true that there is no sort of parity between the properties of the components and the properties of the resultant, but neither was there in the case of the water. It is also true that what I have spoken of as the influence of pre-existing living matter is something quite unintelligible ; but does anybody quite comprehend the *modus operandi* of an electric spark, which traverses a mixture of oxygen and hydrogen ? What justification is there, then, for the assumption of the existence in the living matter of a something which has no representation or correlative in the not living matter which gave rise to it ? What better philosophical status has 'vitality' than 'aquosity' ? And why should vitality hope for a better fate than the other 'itys' which have disappeared since Martinus Scriblerus accounted for the operation of the meat-jack by its inherent 'meat-roasting quality,' and scorned the materialism of those who explained the turning of the spit by a certain mechanism worked by the draught of the chimney ?"

Now, I have very carefully read the whole of Professor Huxley's paper, and this is the only argument I can find for making us believe that there is no such thing in existence as life or vitality beyond the ordinary action of the molecular forces, whatever they may be, when these atoms are brought into a particular state of combination. But the whole of that passage shows the peculiar condition of mind of those naturalists who deny the existence of vitality. He says : " We don't believe that such a thing as 'aquosity' entered into the particles of the oxide of hydrogen when they formed themselves on our windows into those beautiful frosted figures which represent to many minds the appearance and growth of a plant." I have known many persons highly delighted when they have seen under the oxy-hydrogen microscope crystalline forms rushing across the object-glass, and producing in an instant of time the most wonderful vegetable forms, as you would suppose. But that passage betrays the greatest ignorance on the part of Professor Huxley. There is not the slightest analogy on earth between the formation of any crystal and the growth of any plant. He talks of the Protean forms of carbonate of lime : he might also have mentioned the Protean forms of silica. What does he mean by these Protean forms? He means that crystals of carbonate of lime present an enormous variety in the external form of the crystals and in their relation to each other. But, although these forms are bound to each other by certain geometrical laws, no crystalographer whatever could anticipate or prophesy with anything like accuracy whether any particular form could or not be found within certain limits. What takes place in carbonate of lime or silica, or oxide of hydrogen, or any of these crystalline bodies? The greatest diversity of external form, with the greatest possible identity of internal structure. But what have you in a plant? The greatest pertinacity with respect to external form, and at the same time the greatest diversity of internal structure. That is one difference, among many, between living beings and dead crystals. It is a law running through the whole of animated nature that you have the greatest possible diversity of internal constitution of the same plant or animal with the greatest uniformity of external form. In crystals you have the very reverse. But Professor Huxley need not have gone to oxide of hydrogen for his crystals when he had carbon at hand. When pure particles of carbon are allowed to come into contact they will crystallize just as much as the oxide of hydrogen. The diamond is nothing more than a crystal of the pure chemical agent carbon, and no doubt if oxygen, or hydrogen, or nitrogen could be sufficiently cooled or condensed, they would also obey the laws of crystals and crystallize. Similar substances which exist in a solid form do crystallize. We know that phosphorus, sulphur, gold, silver, iron, tin, lead—will crystallize according to certain laws, and there is reason to believe that crystallization is inherent to all dead matter. But when we come in contact with living matter, we come to something very different. Professor Huxley tells us that the great object of his science is to get rid of all these " itys." He wants to know if we can take " aquosity" as a power existing in the water ; and the first illustration he uses is, that if you take oxygen and hydrogen and mix them, they are only a mixture of oxygen and hydrogen, but if you pass an electric spark through them, water is formed. He then asks if I know the *modus operandi* of that electric spark. I say I do not, but the electric spark is not the only thing that will produce that result. Any spark whatever will do it, for there is a law that if the atoms of oxygen and hydrogen, in proper proportions, are brought within a certain nearness of each other, whether by an electric spark or by a common light of any kind, they will combine and form water, that is an ordinary law of nature. If you put into that mixture of oxygen and hydrogen a little piece of a certain description of platinum, all the particles of which are in a spongy state—which allows a kind of capillary attraction, if I may so call it, to operate,—that has the power of bringing the two gases into contact with each other, combination takes place, and you have water formed. In the same way you have only to put into the mixture a piece of pure platinum, provided it is perfectly clean, and the same effect is produced. But is there anything in this at all analogous to living protoplasm? Does it go on producing water? Is there any power in water like that? In the most insignificant form of protoplasm which you can deal with, you find you have something higher than chemical, mechanical, or molecular force. But you have not got rid of all the "itys," even according to Professor Huxley's own illustration. He is obliged to have recourse to the "itys." He takes the oxygen and hydrogen, combining them in certain proportions by their weight: there you have an "ity"—gravity. Then by means of electricity—another "ity"—he gets them to combine, and you have chemical affinity—a third "ity." So that we have three "itys," in his own illustration of the formation of that very thing in reference to which he scoffs at the term "aquosity." He has to admit the existence of three "itys" in that. But this is very important. I think there is something here which might have got the professor out of the slough of materialism, which he told his hearers he had led them into purposely in order that he might afterwards get them out of it. The whole argument of the paper is that, in the present state of modern science, men of science cannot go on in any other way than by using materialistic formulæ, as the only formulæ which will advance science. The spiritualistic formulæ, he says, if true, will not advance science one bit. Now, it is not until the end of the paper that he attempts to get his hearers out of the slough of materialism into which he had purposely led them. Just as he says there is no such thing as vitality, he maintains there is no such thing as human thought, except the mere molecular action of the protoplasm of his brain, and the protoplasm of his hearers' brains sitting in judgment on what he tells them. And yet he says that, after all, he is no materialist; that materialism is utterly ineffectual; and moreover that "systematic materialism may paralyze the energies and destroy the beauty of a life." But he has no way of getting the people out of this slough of materialism, except by speaking contemptuously of all the higher and nobler branches of true philosophy. He says :—

"I bid you beware that, in accepting these conclusions, you are placing your feet on the first rung of a ladder which, in most people's estimation, is the reverse of Jacob's, and leads to the antipodes of heaven. It may seem a small thing to admit that the dull vital actions of a fungus or a foraminifer are the properties of their protoplasm, and are the direct results of the nature of the matter of which they are composed. But if, as I have endeavoured to prove to you, their protoplasm is essentially identical with, and most readily converted into, that of any animal, I can discover no logical halting-place between the admission that such is the case and the further concession that all vital action may, with equal propriety, be said to be the result of the molecular forces of the protoplasm which displays it."

We suppose we are coming to something definite here; but he goes on to tell us, further on, that—

"We can have no knowledge of the nature of either matter or spirit; and the notion of necessity is something illegitimately thrust into the perfectly legitimate conception of law; and the materialistic position, that there is nothing in the world but matter, force, and necessity, is as utterly devoid of justification as the most baseless of theological dogmas. The fundamental doctrines of materialism, like those of spiritualism, and most other 'isms,' lie outside 'the limits of philosophical inquiry,' and David Hume's great service to humanity is his irrefragable demonstration of what these limits are. Hume called himself a sceptic, and therefore others cannot be blamed if they apply the same title to him; but that does not alter the fact that the name, with its existing implications, does him gross injustice. If a man asks me what the politics of the inhabitants of the moon are, and I reply that I do not know; that neither I nor any one else have any means of knowing; and that, under these circumstances, I decline to trouble myself about the subject at all, I do not think he has any right to call me a sceptic. On the contrary, in replying thus, I conceive that I am simply honest and truthful, and show a proper regard for the economy of time. So Hume's strong and subtle intellect takes up a great many problems about which we are naturally anxious, and shows us that they are essentially questions of lunar politics, in their essence incapable of being answered, and therefore not worth the attention of men who have work to do in the world. And he thus ends one of his essays :—' If we take in hand any volume of divinity, or school metaphysics, for instance, let us ask, Does it contain any abstract reasoning concerning quantity or number? No. Does it contain any experimental reasoning concerning matter of fact and existence? No. Commit it, then, to the flames, for it can contain nothing but sophistry and illusion.' "

All he can find to comfort the minds of the changed protoplasm listening to him, is that all high and noble things are mere sophistry and delusion. He might have gone back to his simple illustration of the Protean forms of carbonate of lime, and he might have spoken of silica. We have not got to ascend very high up in the scale of animal creation before we find masses of protoplasm—nothing but the pure protoplasm he speaks of,—apparently homogeneous masses, displaying under the microscope no traces of structure, but only the marvellous movement he speaks of in the protoplasm of the nettle. But what do we find that living—not dead—protoplasm doing? We find it having the power of seizing upon the particles of carbonate of lime with which it comes in contact, while another species of protoplasm seizes on particles of silica, and with them they build up marvellous structures, not of protoplasm, but of pure carbonate of lime, or of pure silica. They elaborate those materials into some of the most beautiful forms you have ever seen under the microscope. You have seen those beautiful pieces of transparent silica, which they have worked upon, giving you, under the microscope, all the apparent markings of an engine-turned watch. And that one species of protoplasm has gone on from the time of its creation, for thousands and thousands of years, building up such masses of silica as those, and elaborating them into those beautiful forms—perfectly uniform in external form—and entirely different from the Protean forms of silica or carbonate of lime crystals. The living protoplasm of one species alone has the power of taking particles of carbonate of lime and building them up into beauteous structures unchanged through thousands of generations. The molecular forces on the other hand uninfluenced by living protoplasm build only Protean forms of crystals having no analogy whatever to the permanent structures produced by living agents. In spite of Darwin's supposed law of progression, Professor Huxley is obliged to admit that these very forms of carbonate of lime and silica, built up by masses of protoplasm, which are but the creatures of a day, perfectly ephemeral—he is obliged to admit that these forms of lime and silica have been left as a token of the living powers of the protoplasm that formed them. All the immense masses of our chalky rocks are the works of these little creatures, whose descendants are forming now, like strata upon the bed of the Atlantic ocean. The deposits, dredged up recently from the depths of the Atlantic, are precisely the same as those found in the white cliffs of Albion, so that there is nothing here to lead us out of the slough. I will not enter upon any details concerning such marvellous structures as the ear, the eye, or the heart of man; but I would ask, Am I to have no curiosity to go beyond the mere operation of molecular forces for such extraordinary formations as these? The wisdom, the marvellous power, the marvellous science shown in these things—surely it must be a branch of pure philosophy to inquire into them. I know what was Newton's philosophy, for he has told us the eye and the ear could not have been formed without wondrous skill in optics and acoustics. But even Professor Huxley admits that there is a something which he cannot get over, but which would have led him out of the slough. He says :—

"We may by-and-by be able to see our way as clearly from the constituents of water to the properties of water, as we are now able to deduce the operations of a watch from the form of its parts and the manner in which they are put together."

Now what does a watch consist of? So much brass, so much steel, perhaps so much gold—but that is only in the ornamental part. There you have the protoplasm. (Laughter.) But I ask you, is that all a watch contains? You say "Yes; all that science can teach you is that a watch contains so many particles of iron, and zinc, and copper." But then these things are very cunningly arranged together; there is a most marvellous cunning in the arrangement of all the parts; and I find the watch does for me that which the earliest of the human race had no knowledge of at all —it keeps accurate time for me by taking advantage not only of molecular forces, but of certain laws of mechanics which it took the human race a very long time to discover. Some one had the wit to discover that a pendulum vibrated pretty evenly in seconds of time, according to its length, and when he wanted to get rid of the burdensome pendulum, he found that a small fine spring of steel which would bend backwards and forwards, would answer the purpose as well, and that this, in conjunction with certain wheels and other works, could be made the means of measuring the time just as accurately as by the pendulum. The watch therefore has something in it beyond the mere protoplasm of iron, zinc, and copper. I must not call it vitality—but it has something in it which does not at all belong to molecular action. And it has a great deal more: there is impressed upon it a certain amount of human wisdom and thought and experience, all, as it were, embodied and contained in it. Am I then to make no inquiry about these things, but put them down at once as mere lunar politics? Is not this as really a true subject of science or philosophy as anything about protoplasms and carbon or hydrogen or nitrogen? But Professor Huxley might have gone further. He says :—

" Why should 'vitality' hope for a better fate than the other 'itys' which have disappeared since Martinus Scriblerus accounted for the operation of the meat-jack by its inherent 'meat-roasting quality,' and scorned the 'materialism' of those who explained the turning of the spit by a certain mechanism worked by the draught of the chimney ?"

Well, it may be that Professor Huxley is too refined a specimen of human intellect to admit the jack as a witness ; but there is the same kind of power displayed in the mechanism of the jack, the same evidence of human thought and invention, mastering the mere material elements and making them work in order to save a man the trouble of turning the spit which turns the meat he desires to roast. By means of a little iron and brass and the smoke of the chimney he is enabled to have the work done which otherwise he would have had to do with his own fingers, to the material detriment and consumption of his own protoplasm. (Laughter.) Professor Huxley laughs at at the man who " scorns the materialism of the jack," and attributes its motion " to its meat-roasting quality." But does its motion come from its materialism, or would it have had that motion if something immaterial had not in the first place been brought to bear upon it ? Here too, however, we are brought back to " human politics " not " lunar politics." (Laughter.) A man boasts that he can send his thoughts through the depths of the Atlantic, and communicate with a continent thousands of miles away by means of that " ity "—electricity. But we do not speak of that as being a matter of materialism—we talk of it as one of the greatest achievements of the human intellect. But if I admit that this is one of the grandest achievements of the human intellect, what must we say of those wonderful electric cables, the nerves of my body, which convey such marvellous sensations to my brain ? They are analogous to the electric apparatus which man makes, but they were not made by man—they were not formed by human wisdom. When man discovered how to make the electric apparatus he found that the electric-eel had already a galvanic battery in its body which no human science has ever been able to imitate. He finds an eel containing a battery sufficiently powerful to convey men's thoughts from the Old World to the New. There it exists in a living form, made by a living protoplasm in the eel. But is that electricity the work of the protoplasm in the body of the eel? No more than the meat-roasting quality of the jack, or the time-keeping quality of the watch, is the work of the brass and iron and other materials of which they are composed. But surely it is not lunar politics which induces us to inquire into these things? What does Professor Huxley's own branch of science—physiology—teach us? Has that been advanced by materialistic formulæ? I maintain that it has not, and that the whole progress of that science gives the lie to what he says when he tells us that the materialistic formulæ alone, and not the spiritualistic formulæ, will make advances in scientific discovery. It was not the materialistic formulæ which led Newton to discover gravitation, for he was searching after the first great cause—after that wisdom displayed in God's works which always worked in the simplest and most beautiful way possible. It was not the materialistic formulæ which led Harvey to discover the circulation of the blood. He told that Christian philosopher, Boyle, that he derived the hint that led to the discovery, from the fact that he found veins had valves in them. He argued that those valves would not have been put there except for use, and their position taught him in which direction the current would flow. Take all the greatest discoveries in physiology, point out one, if you can, which has been discovered by those materialistic formulæ, which would reduce all the works of the Deity to the mere dead operation of mechanical laws. All the greatest discoveries in the mere material world have been made by those who have searched for perfect wisdom in all God's works. Sir Isaac Newton thought it was impossible to make an achromatic telescope, and therefore all that he made were reflecting telescopes, but he was misled by imperfect observation, or by a hasty generalization from the refractive powers of certain salts of lead. But what led to the discovery and the forma-tion of the achromatic telescope was the observation of a man, who said "the instrument which God had made for man to see with must be the perfect instrument." He knew that when he used an unachromatic telescope everything he saw was confused and tinged with various colours, while there was none of that confusion or colouring in the images which were depicted on his own retina. He went directly to God's works, and asked them how it was that the marvellous thing was produced. He found that in the eye there were three different lenses, and that those lenses possessed not only different refractive, but different dispersive powers, and he calculated how, by lenses of different substances, he could imitate imperfectly in the telescope what was perfectly done in the eye. Then the astronomical refracting telescope not only became a possibility, it became an actuality in science. But in all its perfection it is a very long way from the eye, which Darwin supposes to be made without any skill in optics. The eye contains wonders in its construc-tion which the physiologist and physicist have not yet fathomed. With all their skill and power they cannot combine the telescope and microscope in one instrument, and no physiologist has yet been able to tell us what is that marvellous power of the eye by means of which we can see distinctly an object within six or seven inches, and also the furthest star that manifests itself to the vision. Men have had a suspicion that there is a marvellous mechanism doing all this, but they have not been able to read that mechanism yet. Will they read it best by the materialistic formulæ, or by the spiritualistic formulæ, which teaches them that it was made by Him who not only made that optical instrument, but who also made all the laws of optics, and made the two in perfect conformity with each other? You may depend upon it that the highest spiritual philosophy will most advance science, and also be most in accordance with common sense. (Loud cheers.)

WYMAN AND SONS, PRINTERS, GREAT QUEEN STREET, LONDON, W.C.

www.ingramcontent.com/pod-product-compliance
Lightning Source LLC
Chambersburg PA
CBHW081308040426

42452CB00014B/2696